Chicago Theological Seminary

Quarter Centennial Historical Sketch

Chicago Theological Seminary

Quarter Centennial Historical Sketch

ISBN/EAN: 9783337096311

Printed in Europe, USA, Canada, Australia, Japan

Cover: Foto ©ninafisch / pixelio.de

More available books at **www.hansebooks.com**

CHICAGO THEOLOGICAL SEMINARY.

AS PLANNED AND PARTLY BUILT

Chicago Theological Seminary.

QUARTER CENTENNIAL

HISTORICAL SKETCH.

PUBLISHED BY THE BOARD OF DIRECTORS.

CHICAGO.
JAMESON & MORSE, BOOK AND JOB PRINTERS.
1879.

CONTENTS.

STATEMENT.

By the "Great Fire" in Chicago, October, 1871, there were lost the Records of the Board of Directors of the Chicago Theological Seminary, also the Records of their Executive Committee, the official Reports of the Treasurer and Agent, as well as many other important documents. In consequence only a meager History of the Seminary did the Committee, appointed for that purpose, count themselves able to make.

They have, however, been gratefully surprised to find how much reliable history they still could gather. This required minute search in private diaries and letters, in written memoranda, published periodicals and the fortunately preserved duplicates of Reports made by Mr. Kedzie during his Agency, and involved also extensive correspondence.

Often long search and much correspondence has been necessary to settle a date or fact, which could be recorded in a single line. The Committee have spared no pains to make this History accurate. For all important dates and facts they found some printed document, written memorandum, or personal testimony, on which they could rely. Thus they have been able to gather the important facts concerning the organization and work of the Seminary thus far, which, else, were likely to perish with this generation.

A review of those early times awakens conflicting emotions in the minds of those participating therein. The Directors, undertaking a work in which they never

4

before had been engaged, saw, afterward, wherein errors of judgment were committed, for which they found some excuse in their right intent and lack of experience. To bring the Seminary to its present stage of progress, has cost much care and labor on the part of the Directors and Professors — gladly again to be endured for completing a work so well begun.

Upon our Chicago Theological Seminary, this sacred, and, we trust, yet to become ancient seat of learning, we invoke what it has hitherto enjoyed, the coöperation of the churches and the favor of Him, their Divine Head, that thus it may grow to full maturity of strength, and come to ripe, abundant and perpetual fruitage.

A. S. KEDZIE,

Chairman of Committee.

Chicago, Ill., June, 1879.

I.

PLANS FOR THEOLOGICAL STUDY IN WESTERN COLLEGES.

The establishment of colleges in the Northwest was in the interest both of education and religion. Their founders looked forward to educating a christian ministry, as an important function of those colleges. Facilities for theological education were provided in the plan of some of them.

Soon after Beloit College began its work, the question of providing theological education came before its Trustees in consequence of actual application for such instruction. To meet this want, early in 1852 the Pastor elect of the First Congregational Church in Beloit was elected Professor of Theology in the college. This, it was thought, would be the beginning of a Theological Department in which Congregationalists and Presbyterians could unite, and where students in theology would come with advantage under the influence and instruction of a pastor. The call to both offices was declined. No further attempt has been made to open a Theological Department in Beloit College. The large number of young men whom this college has helped train for the ministry, shows that it is fulfilling a noble design in its own proper sphere as a college.

When the attempt was made to found Illinois College there was in a large part of Illinois a violent prejudice against church and clergy—so violent that for two years the Legislature refused a charter for the college. One cause for this hostility was a wide and wild excitement caused throughout the West by Hon. R. M. Johnson's Report in Congress against the Anti-Sunday Mails Petition, charging the petitioners with the design of uniting church and state, and of establishing a religious despotism. Men, whose memories run not back to that time, have little idea of the violence and bitterness of that excitement. Only when, later, four religious denominations united in application for charters, were any granted. The charter of Illinois College, when first granted, forbade theological education: afterward this prohibition was repealed. A legacy was received by the college toward founding a Professorship of Theology. The Trustees, though not making any formal relinquishment of the design, have not, as yet, taken any steps to open a Theological Department.

It was in the original design of Knox College to have a Theological Department, and a fund was set apart for that purpose. Afterward the plan was abandoned, and the fund, according to provision before made, was devoted to the college proper.

When founding a Theological Seminary in Michigan was first discussed, one of the projects under consideration was to have the Seminary located on the campus of the State University, by permission of the Regents, that the theological students might avail themselves of certain courses of instruction in the University, thereby enlarging the range of study, and affording helps to those pursuing a special course of studies.

Iowa College had no place in its plan for a Theological Department: yet the education of ministers was central in the aim of its founders, so far as it could be helped by a thorough course of collegiate study. The history of the college and its work of helping men into the ministry show how well the founders of the college planned and wrought.

The same may be said of Carlton, Wheaton, Olivet, Ripon and other colleges, which have come into prominence since Chicago Theological Seminary was founded. Their most precious fruit is the young men they educate for the ministry.

But in respect to those colleges which had theological education in their plans, it was seen that to lay their foundations, involved struggles so many, that, though none of them came to founding a Theological Department, their success as colleges was ample reward and honor for the heroic faith of their founders. Besides, another and better design seems to have been in the purpose of God, as disclosed by His providences, the establishment of one Theological Seminary, uniting all the Congregational churches in the Northwest.

II.

BEGINNINGS.

Plans for theological education not having come to maturity in the colleges, from the year 1850 to 1860 there was a general move among evangelical denominations in the Northwest for theological education. This led to the establishment of theological seminaries.* The discussion

* The "Garrett Biblical Institute" of the Methodists was opened in Sept., 1856;—the "Chicago Theological Seminary" of the Congregationalists in Oct., 1858;—the "Presbyterian Theological Seminary of the Northwest" in Oct., 1859, it having been transferred from New Albany, Ind. —and the "Baptist Union Theological Seminary" in Oct., 1867, though theological instruction had been given during the two previous years under the auspices of the Baptist Theological Union.

incident thereto led many men of broad views and catholic spirit to favor the union of Presbyterians and Congregationalists in one theological seminary. This was resisted by men of more intense denominational affinities. The resistance came principally from the Presbyterians, who had the advantages of early occupation and greater strength. The Congregationalists, pressed with a sense of responsibility to do their share of the work of evangelization in the Northwest, continued to grope their way for the path, which at length they found.

The design of founding a Theological Seminary in the Northwest came, about the same time, to different Congregationalists, though far removed from each other. This may show it all the more clearly to have been "what the spirit saith to the churches."

Previous to 1853 the need of a larger supply of ministers for the smaller churches in Michigan, and of men more adequately trained for pastoral work, occupied the attention of thoughtful men in that State. To meet this want the plan of theological education, indicated below, was designed by Rev. L. Smith Hobart, then pastor at Ann Arbor, and by him submitted to the General Association of Michigan, in May, 1853. This plan was given into the hands of a committee of the Association, Messrs. H. D. Kitchel, A. S. Kedzie and D. Mussey, who reported it to that body for favorable consideration. After discussion it was referred to a committee, Revs. L. Smith Hobart, E. N. Bartlett and J. Patchin, for report at the next annual meeting.

The chairman of this committee sent a copy of the Plan to the Congregational Herald, which was published in its issue of June 18th, 1853. It awakened interest among the ministers of the Northwest, many of whom, during that year, came to feel that efforts should soon be made to found a Theological Seminary in this large and important section of our country. When first designed the plan was to have a Theological Seminary in Michigan and chiefly for that State. But further study and a correspondence which revealed the broader plan entertained by the brethren in Illinois—to have one Seminary for the Northwest—led to a ready acquiescence therein.

At the next meeting of the General Association of Michigan, at Detroit, May, 1854, this committee made report, calling attention to the fact that the Plan proposed sought to combine the advantages of two methods of theological education, study with pastors and instruction in a seminary. The Plan embraced the following particulars:—The establishment of a Theological Seminary at some eligible point in the Northwest:—its course of study to be divided, each year, into two terms, a Lecture Term of six months under the instruction of the Faculty, and a Reading Term of six months, to be pursued with pastors of churches:—The degree of Bachelor of Divinity to be conferred on those completing the full course of study:—Each State interested in the Seminary to endow a Professorship:—The control of the Institution to be in a Board of Trustees elected by the General Association of such States:—Contributions to be taken up annually in the churches for the Library.

After full discussion the General Association adopted the report of the Committee, highly approving its Plan of a Theological Seminary, and authorized the Secretary to confer with other Ecclesiastical Bodies in the Northwest to secure their approval and coöperation.

Accordingly, the Secretary, Rev. L. S. Hobart, communicated with ministers in the Northwest on the subject.

He also furnished a copy of the report to Rev. H. L.
Hammond, delegate to the General Association of Iowa,
which was laid before that body at Davenport, June, 1854,
and received its hearty approval.

Meantime, the roots which have given growth to
Chicago Theological Seminary, were germinating else-
where. It was an encouragement to the founders of the
Seminary that its roots spread so far.

In March, 1854, Rev. Stephen Peet, of Batavia, Ills.,
and Rev. G. S. F. Savage, of St. Charles, Ills., after con-
ferring with each other, sent letters to several brethren in
Wisconsin and Illinois, calling a meeting to consider the
project of founding a Theological Seminary for the Northwest. This meeting was held two weeks later in Chicago,
Philo Carpenter, Esq., being Moderator, and Rev. G. S. F.
Savage, Scribe. The result of discussion was a unani-
mous conviction that the project was important and
feasible. An adjourned meeting was held a few weeks
later, in which Iowa was represented, and the movement
in Michigan reported.

As a result of deliberations at this adjourned meeting
and at the State Associations following, a larger meeting
was called. It met in Chicago June 12th, 1854, with Rev.
Asa Turner, Jr., of Iowa, for Moderator, and Rev. G. S. F.
Savage, Scribe. Most of the Northwestern States were
represented. Discussion in this meeting revealed the
fact, that its members, often without conference, had been
deeply interested in founding a Theological Seminary in
the Northwest. This meeting voted that the time had
fully come for this work, and elected a committee of
twenty-one, from Illinois, Indiana, Michigan, Wisconsin,
Iowa, Missouri and Minnesota, to mature the Plan of the
Seminary; to invite proposals for a central site; to make

other preliminary arrangements and submit the same to a general convention of Congregationalists in the Northwest, to meet in Chicago upon call of said committee.

This committee of twenty-one met in Chicago, July 12th, 1854. After a full comparison of views and discussion of measures, it was voted to call a convention of those interested in founding a Theological Seminary, to meet at Chicago in the following September. Meanwhile, in timely utterances, the project was held before the churches by Rev. J. C. Holbrook, in the Congregational Herald, of which he was editor.

In faith that the churches would approve the enterprise and in anticipation of future organization, friends of the project, as early as June, 1854, secured the services of Rev. S. Peet as Financial Agent, holding themselves responsible to him for an annual salary of $1,200 and traveling expenses.

The Seminary was conceived in many hearts, longed for in many prayers. It was demanded by increasing destitutions and by multiplication of churches, as the wave of population rolled westward and spread into hitherto uninhabited wastes. A movement to found the Seminary, once begun, called out the deep interest felt on the subject in minds widely separated, not stirred by mutual talk, but because they had talked much with God about the moral influence and destiny of these Northwestern States.

That there was to be a Theological Seminary in the Northwest, was a foregone conclusion. Christian homes, churches and colleges prepared the way for it. These Christian forces, for full development and free work, needed to become productive of a ministry. Their full-orbed life could not else be reached. The elements of a Christian civilization were at work over these broad

States, and all the agencies of such a civilization were to
be brought forth and put to use.

Besides, here were gathering mighty forces: some of
them hostile to Christ's sovereignty over these common-
wealths and their teeming populations. In the coming
conflicts no agencies of the Gospel could be spared, least
of all the Savior's ascension gift, the Gospel ministry.

III.

ORGANIZATION.

The Convention called by the before named Committee
of twenty-one, met at Chicago Sept. 26th, 1854, in the
Plymouth Church, and was attended by delegates from
the churches in Michigan, Indiana, Illinois, Iowa, Wisconsin and Missouri. The first question in this Convention was whether the time had come for our churches to
found a Theological Seminary. Both "No" and "Yes"
were given in answer. The judgment of other churches,
expressed by movements for this end, already begun, had
its influence. It was felt by many that our churches
could not be what their times and surroundings require,
unless productive of a ministry. It was no objection to
the project that there were ministers out of employ; for
not salaries unused, but work undone, was the matter to
be looked after. Some held that our 380 churches in
the Northwest were hardly an adequate constituency for
a Theological Seminary. The faith of others, however,
saw a large increase of this number in the near future.

Under this expectation, the Convention ratified the action of preliminary meetings and elected a Board of Directors—the charter members of the Board, distributed among the States as follows: –

MICHIGAN.—Rev. L. Smith Hobart, Rev. Harvey D. Kitchel, Rev. Adam S. Kedzie, Judge Solomon L. Withey, and Joseph E. Beebe, Esq.

ILLINOIS.—Rev. Stephen Peet, Rev. William Carter, Rev. Flavel Bascom, Rev. George W. Perkins, Rev. John C. Holbrook, Rev. Nathaniel H. Eggleston, Rev. George S. F. Savage, Philo Carpenter, Esq., and Joseph Johnston, . Esq.

IOWA.—Rev. Alden B. Robbins, Rev. Jesse Gurnsey, and John G. Foote, Esq.

WISCONSIN.—Rev. Charles W. Camp, Rev. Hiram Foote, Rev. John J. Miter, and Horace Hobart, Esq.

MINNESOTA.—Rev. Richard Hall.

INDIANA.—Rev. M. Augustas Jewett.

MISSOURI.—Rev. Truman M. Post.

The first Board of Visitors were Rev. Asa Turner, Jr., of Iowa; Rev. N. C. Clark, Rev. R. M. Pearson and A. Comstock, Esq., of Illinois; Rev. H. N. Brinsmade and Rev. S. M. Eaton, of Wisconsin; and Rev. D. M. Bardwell, of Indiana.

The Board of Directors were organized Sept. 27, 1854, by electing Rev. S. Peet, President; Rev. N. H. Eggleston, Scribe; Philo Carpenter, Esq., Treasurer; Rev. S. Peet, Rev. J. C. Holbrook, Rev. G. W. Perkins, Philo Carpenter, Esq., and Joseph Johnston, Esq., Executive Committee; which Committee were instructed to procure a Charter. Rev. L. S. Hobart, Rev. A. S. Kedzie and Rev. H. D. Kitchel were elected a Committee to draft a Constitution, which work providentially fell to the second member of the Committee, he having frequent consultations with the others.

In this Convention and in the early meetings of the Board of Directors to the Seminary its characteristic features were given. Of these none were deemed of greater importance than the control, under which the Seminary should be. A close and self-perpetuating corporation was advocated by some and opposed by more. The original plan of having the Board of Control elected by the General Associations was advocated, and then opposed on the ground that such Associations were human institutions, which probably would continue, but might not. The churches, on the other hand, were held to be of divine institution; and that the Seminary would be best cared for, most successfully nurtured, as well as most effectually guarded against error, if put under the watch and control of the churches. This view after full discussion prevailed with unanimity; and the election of Directors and Visitors was, by the Convention, and by the consequent provisions of the Constitution, put into the hands of the churches interested, meeting for this purpose in Triennial Convention.

The Convention held that for sufficient reasons they could make the Seminary different from any other. Some felt that there should be a more practical way of training men for their work, as found in the legal and medical professions; and that ministers should not, as so often, by continuous scholastic study, be educated out of acquaintance and sympathy with the conditions, in which they were to work. This view was advocated by Rev. L. S. Hobart and Rev. S. Peet. To teach it was original; nor to them alone. With more or less distinctness the same convictions stirred in the minds of many Western Ministers, started by a desire to reach the people, for which they felt their scholastic habits had somewhat unfitted them.

This led to the adoption of what has been called the "Reading Term," found afterwards to be a misnomer. The original design contemplated a course of reading to be pursued by each student under the instruction of some pastor. But a more important end was to be served by initiating the student into the practical work of his calling under the guidance of an experienced pastor, engaging with him in pastoral visitation and in other forms of ministerial work.

But the Lord seems to call many to the ministry, who are not rich in this world's goods. This fact and lack of adequate scholarship-funds have led to a practical modification of this Reading Term, in which, however, some of its most valuable features are still retained. Students take charge of vacant churches and get much valuable training by these experimental ministrations. A modification of the original plan may be demanded by the necessities of the case, and it still be retained as a characteristic and valuable feature of the Seminary.

In this Convention some urged a Special Course of study by which men, too old to go through college, or for other reasons unable to do so, yet nevertheless having had advantages of study, and having withal a heart devoted to the work, and natural gifts therefor, might be educated for the ministry. This course was advocated by Rev. J. C. Holbrook, suggested, perhaps, by his own successful experience, as the course of other christian denominations had suggested to many minds. The Convention authorized this department of the Seminary's work; and the usefulness of the men, who have thereby

been educated for the ministry, has amply justified the
wisdom of the Convention. In its essential features this
course of study has been adopted by other theological
seminaries. For a full discussion of the subject reference
is made to a Report thereon to the Triennial Convention
of 1879.

An enlargement in the curriculum of theological
study was advocated in the Convention. Though favorably received, no action was taken. Subsequently the
matter came up in the early meetings of the Board of
Directors. They held that the ministers needed in the
West, while panoplied in Biblical Doctrine, must be able
to meet those who rejected every appeal to the Bible; and
that the students sent forth from this Seminary must be
fitted for a more varied campaign, than they would be
qualified for under the old routine of theological study.
And this view still has a strong hold among the Directors.
It has led at different times to the introduction of Special
Lectures, as need and ability warranted—an example followed, also, by other Seminaries.

A final subject considered in the Convention was coöperation with the New School Presbyterians of the
Northwest in founding a Union Theological Seminary.
When these Presbyterians in 1850 and later had in hand
the plan of founding at Galena, Chicago or elsewhere, a
Theological Seminary for the Northwest, they declined
an overture for making it a Union Seminary in which
Congregationalists and Presbyterians would have equal
rights, powers and privileges. This overture was declined,
doubtless for what seemed to them good reasons. Such
copartnership might subsequently have stood in the way
of a union of the two General Assemblies.

Long wonted to coöperate with Presbyterians in Home and Foreign Missions, as also in other benevolent enterprises, Congregationalists still kept alive the amiable spirit of the disowned " Plan of Union." In consequence, after much discussion, the Convention instructed the Board of Directors to entertain favorably any proposition for denominational union in the work of training men for the ministry. The Directors even went further, took the initiative and privately proposed such coöperaation with the New School Presbyterians, which, however, was unofficially declined. Union in the work of theological education will doubtless come as a fruit of a broader charity and a more perfect union among evangelical churches.

IV.

ACTION OF GENERAL ASSOCIATIONS.

Though the Board of Directors were upborne by the enthusiasm of the Convention electing them, yet they felt solicitous for votes of confidence, which the churches might give in the calm deliberation of their State Associations. It would be repetitious to place all their "Resolutions" upon record. Representative illustrations are here given, pertaining to the Seminary as a projected design, and then as an actual organization. This chapter might be enlarged by recording the favorable action of these Associations from year to year according to the various conditions of the Seminary's want and work.

In May, 1854, the General Association of Michigan, anticipating the founding of a Theological Seminary and having the plan of it already before them, "RESOLVED—That we adopt the report of the committee, highly approving the Plan of a Theological Seminary which is proposed therein, and that we authorize the Secretary to confer with other Ecclesiastical Bodies in the Northwest for the purpose of securing its approval by them, and the adoption of such measures as may be necessary for the accomplishment of the end in view."

The date of this action and the fact, that it was taken upon the report of a committee appointed the year before, show how early the churches in Michigan gave attention to this matter.

In the autumn of the same year the General Convention of Presbyterian and Congregational churches in Wisconsin on this subject took action, which shows how reluctant some were to abandon the idea of a Union Seminary. Their action was as follows:

"*Whereas*, the subject of establishing Theological Seminaries in the Northwest has for some time past been under consideration by individuals and ecclesiastical bodies, and preliminary steps have been taken toward establishing two such Institutions in Chicago;—And *Whereas* such movements are of great importance to the interests of religion among us:

"RESOLVED—That it is the opinion of this Convention that immediate and efficient measures should be taken to furnish in the Northwest theological instruction suited to the wants of christian young men desirous to enter the ministry.

"RESOLVED—That in view of the numbers and condition of the Theological Institutions at the East, the churches at the West cannot at present reasonably depend on the munificence of their Eastern Brethern, but should rely mainly on their own resources for the means to provide theological instruction for our young men.

"RESOLVED—That in the opinion of this Convention one Theological Institution is all that will be needful for many years to come in the Northwest for Congregationalists and New School Presbyterians; and that to undertake a distinctive Congregational or Presbyterian Seminary in the Northwest would be unwise and injurious to the best interests of Christ's Kingdom in this region.

"RESOLVED—That we hereby declare our sincere desire for a union of the two denominations in providing Theological instruction, and that we are ready to pledge our hearty co-operation in such an enterprise."

Subsequently President Chapin of Beloit college wrote:—"The course of events rendered such a joint enterprise impracticable, and the Convention in due time came heartily to the recommendation and support of the Chicago Theological Seminary, and has contributed freely to its establishment and operations."

From the minutes of the General Association of Iowa for 1854, the following extract is made:—"A Report on the subject of theological education in the Northwest was made by a Delegate from the General Association of Michigan;" whereupon the Association—

"RESOLVED—That we approve of the establishment at an early day of a Theological Institution in the Northwest, according to the general principles proposed in the Report." Next year they—

"RESOLVED—That we feel strong confidence in the wisdom of the plan for establishing a Theological Seminary at Chicago; that we are deeply interested in its prosperity, and hereby pledge our prayers and active coöperation for the accomplishment of the enterprise."

The minutes of the General Association of Illinois for 1855, say:—"An efficient movement has been begun for a Theological Seminary to be located at Chicago, and the institution is expected soon to be placed on a permanent basis." The next year in their narrative of the state of religion they say:—"A wide spread interest has been awakened in the establishment of the Chicago Theological Seminary, and a ready response has been made to efforts to give it a full endowment and efficient support. We heartily commend this Institution to the confidence and prayers of the churches as an important and essential instrument in raising up a ministry for the West."

These Associations and others in the Northwest during subsequent years have expressed their interest in the Seminary, their approval of its men and methods, their sympathy in its trials, and their satisfaction in its graduates.

V.

STRUGGLES OF PREPARATION.

The Board of Directors met at Chicago, March 27, 1855, in deep sorrow, because of the sudden death of Rev. S. Peet, their President and Financial Agent. Some of them had individually co-operated with him in his successful labors for the Seminary; the others had heard of his success, and been quickened by his enthusiasm. In the interest of the Seminary he went to New England, where he found the project looked upon with curiosity by some and with deep interest by many. To report results he called a meeting of the Board, in the hope that what had been so auspiciously begun would soon be completed. The sanguine hopes of many, the headlong rush of Western life, and an inadequate sense of the cost of a Theological Seminary, led many to look for the opening of the Seminary—even if in a somewhat immature condition— at least as early as during the next autumn, there having then been a whole year of preparation!

Could the Board have seen that three and a half years of struggle still awaited them before the realization of their hopes in the actual work of the Seminary, though their faith might not have failed, yet the sadness of their meeting would have been deeper. But prayer and conference brought them to the conviction, that the design of founding this Theological Seminary was born, not in the counsel of men, but in the wisdom of God: and that He still called them to a vigorous prosecution of the work.

Moved with this conviction, the Board, without faltering, pushed on their work. Mr. Carpenter declining to serve as Treasurer because of the press of his own business, the Board elected Lucius D. Olmsted, Esq., to that office, which he held till his death, in March, 1862, discharging its complicated and onerous duties with success, yet without reward, save the satisfaction of aiding in what he considered an important work of his life. Reasonably, the Board paid for the clerk service needed in the office, the collection of funds from subscribers being chiefly by correspondence.

For Financial Agent, Rev. Adam S. Kedzie, of Michigan, was chosen. He soon entered upon the work and continued it till July, 1862, canvassing most of the Congregational Churches of the Northwest in solicitation of funds, and rendering a varied service in getting the Seminary into working order.

A very favorable Charter was secured without difficulty from the Legislature of Illinois. This Charter, by
recent decision of the Supreme Court of the United
States, exempts all property of the Seminary in Illinois
from taxation. The Directors organized under this
Charter, amended and adopted the Constitution reported
by the Committee, and elected officers. The Charter and
Constitution were printed and distributed, thus making
known more fully the aims and methods of the Seminary·
In so doing, the Constitution was stereotyped, in blessed
ignorance of the fact that the well nigh yearly amend-
ments to it would not let it stay stereotyped.

The finances of the Seminary were found without
order. No system of keeping accounts had been adopted,
nor any books opened. Some of its counted assets were
only verbal promises to give; and others, though in
written form, had no legal validity. The Treasurer and
Agent gave immediate attention to getting affairs into
order, and legal forms into use.

Then began the persistent work of securing funds.
This was chiefly by creating a General Fund, to be ex-
pended for any uses of the Seminary. The plan was to
put the Seminary into operation as soon as possible, and
to meet the cost thereof out of this General Fund, till
endowments were secured, a plan eventually carried out.

Could this increase of assets have gone on as successfully as in 1855 and '56, the Seminary would have
speedily reached prosperity. But soon came the commercial disasters of 1857, which put the Seminary through a
process of seasoning, hardening it for the endurance it
was yet to suffer.

As this was not foreseen, the Executive Committee,
in March, 1856, sent Revs. H. D. Kitchel and A. S. Ked-

zie to the East for wise men to fill the chairs of instruction in the Seminary. Men were freely recommended as Professors, sometimes with a surprising lack of discrimination.

After their return the Board, in April, 1856, elected a Faculty of five Professors for the usual departments of instruction, and enlarged the range of study by electing six lecturers—in expectation that the Seminary would be opened in the autumn of 1856. When, two years later, the Seminary did open, it was with a Faculty able in their personal and professional qualifications, but more economical in numbers.

The difficulties about the location of the Seminary— explained below—lack of funds in the treasury and other facts of incompleteness, made the opening of the Seminary in the autumn of that year, to many of the Directors, seem premature. Such an opening was soon made impracticable by the Professors declining to accept the positions offered them, except one who held his appointment under consideration.

Another election of Professors was made in January, 1857, for the two other most important chairs, in the hope of opening the Seminary in the autumn of that year. But soon throughout the country came the financial disasters which marked 1857. Then doubts arose as to the practicability of opening the Seminary that autumn, and the two Professors newly elected declined. The Board felt strong pressure from subscribers to the funds; some of whom declined further investments till they had returns in the shape of a class graduated from the Seminary. Still, for reasons that seemed imperative to a majority of the Directors, but against the protest of some, the opening of the Seminary was deferred, yet definitely fixed for the autumn of 1858.

In preparation for this the Board of Directors, at
their meeting in April, 1858, elected Rev. Joseph Haven,
D. D., to the chair of Systematic Theology, and Rev.
Samuel C. Bartlett, D. D., to the chair of Biblical Literature. Prof. Franklin W. Fisk, D. D., was, in April,
1856, elected to the chair of Sacred Rhetoric. He held
it a matter of honor to give Beloit College a year's notice
before vacating his chair in that Institution. Accordingly
he was requested by the Directors, in 1858, to give such
notice, so as to occupy his chair in the Seminary as early as
the opening of its second year. These Professors accepted their appointments, and the annual prospect of opening the Seminary stood out as a brighter vision than at
any former time.

VI.

OPENING OF THE SEMINARY.

At last, after four years of preparatory struggle, on
the 6th of October, 1858, the Chicago Theological Seminary was formally opened in the parlors of the First
Congregational Church on the south-west corner of West
Washington and Green streets. The Faculty present
consisted of two Professors, Rev. Joseph Haven, D. D.,
and Rev. Samuel C. Bartlett, D. D. Ten students were
in attendance. A violent rain prevailed during that and
the previous hour, which kept some students, then in dis-
tant parts of the city, from being present. Some of the

Board of Directors, came to see the fulfillment of their long cherished hopes.

The General Agent called the meeting to order and introduced Prof. Haven, who inaugurated the work with a prayer befitting the occasion. It referred to the present day of small things, and then Faith, with her clear and far reaching eye, took into view the future record which the Seminary was to make. Petitions were offered that among the forces then and there set at work, the life of Christ might be central and all-pervading, and that, in gathering their sympathies around the Seminary, the churches might be lifted up into a commanding sympathy with Christ and into a broad field of coöperation with Him.

Brief remarks were made by the Professors and Directors, all in the line of gratefully recognizing the way in which the Lord had guided the affairs of this Institution; and examination of students was assigned for an hour the next day. Among all the doings in that busy, bustling city, the opening of this Theological Seminary was the most significant thing for that day.

At the meeting of the Faculty and students the next day for prayers, Prof. Bartlett officiated, reading the 12th chapter of Romans. Sixteen students were present, and when the Seminary got fairly at work their number was found to be twenty-nine. The Seminary having no buildings, the students were distributed into christian families, by whom, during the first year, they were entertained, in many cases, without charge.

VII.

LOCATION.

The Charter provided that the "Seminary shall be located in or near the City of Chicago." At the first, Mr. Peet made a verbal agreement with the Trustees of Rush Medical College to purchase their building for the use of the Seminary, but this failed.

At the beginning of his agency, Mr. Kedzie was charged with the duty of securing a location for the Seminary. He received a large number of proposals from property owners and real estate dealers, and examined some forty different locations, in quantities varying from one hundred feet square to eighty acres, and in position reaching from central parts of the city to miles away.

To go to some near-by village where location and building for the public rooms of the seminary could be had without cost; to secure a considerable quantity of land for use and sale and build up a suburban town; or to get the best location in the city and put the Seminary in close contact with its churches; these were the projects discussed, often and earnestly. The latter project prevailed, and purchase was made in 1856 of the corner west of Ashland Avenue and south of West Lake street, relying on local interest to help in making payments. This reliance failed, and business was found crowding on that corner. So exchange was made for the entire front of the next block south, facing on Union Park, in 1858.

Payment on this location gave the Directors their sorest financial embarrassment. Inability to make overdue collections brought the Seminary into peril. Hence the depressing influence felt and exerted by the Triennial

Convention of 1861. As on other occasions, from this distress the Seminary was rescued by such friends as Philo Carpenter, C. G. Hammond, E. W. Blatchford, J. M. Williams, T. M. Avery and S. M. Moore. Others in their way tugged at this work as they were able, and their names are not forgotten by Him, for whose dear sake they did it. This relief saved to the Seminary only the south 75 feet of its location, on which then stood its temporary building. This location, though inadequate, being free from incumbrance, was highly prized.

Its inadequacy, however, led to further inquiry and endeavor. At the meeting of the Board of Directors, in April, 1865, Philo Carpenter, Esq., who so often had helped the Board over hard places, came again to their relief. He offered to take the corner on Ashland Avenue and West Washington street, and give in exchange the corner west of Ashland and north of Warren Avenues, fronting on Union Park. Thereby was secured for the Seminary an adequate and permanent location. The remainder of the park-front in this block is owned and used by the Union Park Congregational Church, whose building and those of the Seminary are made to harmonize in style and structure, thereby each adding to the beauty of the other. This exchange involved a gift of $7,000, at prices then current. And this was understood between Mr. Carpenter and the Board to be in lieu of his former conditional gift of $5,000 to the Professorship of Ecclesiastical History. The Board, gratefully recognizing the liberality of Mr. Carpenter, then and previously, voted to call the main building to be erected on that site "Carpenter Hall." So, after much and sore tribulation (more fully shown below in the section on "General Funds,") the Directors came into possession of a location, which, when the buildings are completed, will be adequate, perhaps for generations, and which may be regarded as fitting and beautiful.

In the matter of personal services, mention should be made of the Boards of Directors and Visitors, who, within a wide circle, reaching from Detroit to Indianapolis, St. Louis, Grinnell, Minneapolis and Milwaukee, have at great personal sacrifice, been prompt in attendance at their several and many meetings. They have come together not to ratify plans previously formulated, but have taken all the interests of the Seminary into full consideration, giving them protracted and laborious study, and then handling them as best they could.

The most difficult and perplexing details of their work have been passed over to the Executive Committee, and in managing them this committee have given such service as could be obtained only for the reward of helping so important an interest as the Redeemer's Kingdom.

Mention should also be made of the Board of Auditors, who, annually, have taken up the numerous accounts of the treasury, giving them full investigation and ascertaining their exact condition before reporting them to the Board of Directors with approval—all this gratuitously and as a work of love.

A gratitude which burdens the hearts of many friends of the Seminary, would be denied expression if no mention were made of the sacrifices borne and the efforts made by friends of the Seminary who have had much to do in looking after its pecuniary interests. As elsewhere noted, Philo Carpenter has repeatedly shown himself an active and liberal friend of the Seminary. Among others, mention should also be made of C. G. Hammond, E. W. Blatchford, and J. W. Scoville, who, as liberal donors to

the Seminary, have repeatedly brought it opportune relief in gifts of money and wisdom. The two latter also
as a Financial Committee of the Executive Committee,
have rendered a laborious and invaluable service in advis-
ing the Treasurer as to making investments, and in aiding
him to secure those imperiled by financial depression. If
particulars could be given, a grateful sense of this obligation would be widely felt.

VIII.

BUILDINGS.

The Seminary found its earliest home in the parlors
of the First Congregational Church of Chicago. These
as chapel, lecture and recitation rooms it used, till they
were found inadequate. This church, in 1859, offered to
the Seminary the use for five years of an unfinished mission
building standing a few blocks west of Union Park. This
was accepted and removed to the corner of Ashland Avenue and West Washington street. To it were added the
rooms most urgently needed. This building was for the
use of the Seminary, and those who afterward were organized into the Union Park Congregational Church. To
this church, from its infancy, the Professors of the Seminary ministered, for nearly seven years, till its first pastor, Rev. C. D. Helmer, came—thereby not only eking
out a living which the treasury of the Seminary failed to
afford, but also fostering a church, which in its maturity
became, like the First Church, a nursing mother to the
Seminary.

Meantime it was found impracticable to do without dormitories. The difficulty of having students scattered into different parts of the city, hindering the maintenance of the essential *esprit du corps*, led to renting part of the Union Park Hotel, which in 1864 was used by the students for dormitories.

The location of the Seminary having been removed to the corner of Ashland and Warren Avenues, opportunity was afforded for the erection of permanent buildings, which were demanded by the growth of the institution.

Willard Keyes, Esq., of Quincy, Illinois, having given a block of land in that city toward endowing the Professorship of Ecclesiastical History, consented that the avails of it might be used in the erection of a Hall. This first permanent building, "Keyes Hall," was completed in the autumn of 1865. Besides rooms for general use, it contains studies and dormitories for 38 students. When completed it was not able to meet the wants created by the growth of the Seminary.

In 1868 was begun the erection of the north wing of the main building, called "Carpenter Hall," in acknowledgment of obligation to Philo Carpenter, hitherto the most liberal and opportune donor to the Seminary. In 1869 it was ready for use, and contains a chapel, lecture room and twenty suites of rooms for students. Most of the dormitories and studies in both these halls have been comfortably furnished by churches or individuals. In the erection of these buildings a debt was incurred, which long has been a weight upon the Seminary, and now amounts to $18,600.

LIBRARY.

So important is a library to a Theological Seminary, that steps were taken to secure one for the Chicago Seminary before it was opened. In 1856 the valuable library of Rev. Geo. W. Perkins, containing 500 volumes, was accepted from his estate as payment of his donation of $500 to the Seminary. Valuable gifts of books were secured by Rev. Wm. Patton, D. D., of New Haven, Ct., while traveling in England. Contributions of books were made by Revs. Prof. Twining, J. L. Corning, G. S. F. Savage, D. D., G. F. Magoun, D. D., J. P. Gulliver, D. D., L. Parker, G. B. Hubbard, L. Farnham, A. S. Kedzie, A. W. Porter, R. M. Pearson, T. G. Brainard, H. H. Morgan, and others; also by A. Kingman, Esq., of Boston, Mass., R. Carter and D. Appleton, Esqs., of New York city; James Reed, Esq., of Stockbridge, Mass.; Rev. D. Wilson, of Port Byron, N. Y.; Warren F. Draper, of Andover, Mass., and by Rev. E. N. Kirk, D. D., of Boston, Mass., the last being Walton's Pollyglott Bible, in eight folio volumes, worth $250.

Prof. Bartlett, while Librarian, secured donations, principally from New England Church of Chicago, to the amount of nearly $1000, for the purchase of new and much needed books. In 1875 Rev. E. M. Williams, of Minneapolis, Minn., an alumnus of the Seminary, made a donation of books costing $1,500. These are rare and valuable books, pertaining to Egyptology, and are highly prized by scholars.

The Seminary has thus come to have a library containing some 5,500 volumes, and worth about $7,000.

This is a short story. Would that there were more to tell No want of the Seminary is more imperative than a large increase of the library, and a suitable building in which it can be safely kept. A large and well selected library would strengthen the future ministers of our Northwestern churches for coming conflicts. Besides, it would be an armory from which they might draw weapons, upon occasion, both for defense and attack. Would that some might place within reach of these ministers the critical research and sanctified wisdom of the world's scholarship!

X.

TRIENNIAL CONVENTIONS.

Since the first Convention, which selected the charter members of the Board of Directors, eight Triennial Conventions have been held, averaging 208 members, and representing seven states. Could the names of these members be given, they would be found a fair representation of those who are most earnest and aggressive in pushing the conquests of the Redeemer's Kingdom. These conventions, by their conduct of affairs, have fully justified their having oversight of the Seminary.

Pains have been taken by the different Boards of the Seminary to bring before these conventions a full and accurate statement of its affairs. These statements have been taken up by the conventions in an intelligent way and appreciative spirit. To them they gave full consideration and free discussion. Where difficulty was found and help needed, the delegates to these conventions have not only devised such plans of relief as their wisdom suggested, but have gone back to their churches to carry out these plans—though not always with success—and to quicken the churches with new interest in the Seminary. Thereby the churches have had not only confidence in the conduct of the Seminary's affairs, but also a growing interest in its welfare; and so the conviction has come to them that, in laying its foundations, "they builded better than they knew."

It is no objection to this view, but in illustration of it, that the Second Triennial Convention, held October, 1861, was depressing in its influence upon the minds of the Professors, Directors and friends of the Seminary. This convention was held during the first year of the war of the Rebellion. The finances of the Seminary were in their most depressed condition. The trouble about the location was in its most discouraging stage. In some minds there was lack of faith in the future success of the Seminary; just as in some minds there was lack of faith in the stability of our national government.

But, as in that crisis of our country there were not wanting brave and loyal hearts in adequate numbers, so in that crisis of our Seminary there were not wanting true and fast friends, whose faith in the Seminary—in its work and in its future—wavered not. The Board of Directors made a full exhibit of its affairs, because they had faith in the churches, and in God. Thereby and through help of the convention, they secured the confidence of the churches, as could have been done by no other method.

No one can look over the minutes of these eight conventions; can see how faithfully and fully the condition of the Seminary has been presented by its Boards of Control, Oversight and Instruction, even when some aspects of the condition were full of discouragement;

and can see how fully the presentation has been taken up, discussed until fully understood, and then shaped by the wisdom of the convention, without coming to the conviction that a higher than human wisdom gave the oversight of the Seminary to these Triennial Conventions.

XI.

PROPOSED UNION WITH OBERLIN.

The aim of the Board of Directors was not simply to build up an Institution, but to train men for the ministry. For this, as they had before shown in their willingness to coöperate with New School Presbyterians, they were ready to adopt any coöperative yet efficient means. So, attempt was made, and repeated, to unite Chicago Theological Seminary and the Theological Department of Oberlin College. Though nothing came of it, yet record of these attempts is here made, as showing the spirit of the Board of Directors.

In November, 1857, the Agent, without any formal action of the Board, but in accordance with their wishes, went to Oberlin and informally consulted with some of the Trustees of that college, with Professors in the Theological Department, and with others, on removing that Department with its Professors to Chicago and making it the nucleus of the Theological Seminary then about to be opened there.

Refusals of Professors elect to accept Chairs in the Seminary, led the Board to be less sanguine than at the first, in their hopes of securing men fitted for the work of instruction, and for giving the Seminary a commanding position in the esteem of the churches. In consequence, they were disposed to take men who had already proved themselves competent for these purposes. Hence, the above proposal for union. And though no action was taken by either party, the attempt, though for other reasons, was afterwards renewed in a more formal way.

In June, 1869, Hon. C. G. Hammond, Revs. A. S. Kedzie and H. Foote, members of the Board, were sent to Oberlin, bearing a formal proposal for the transfer of the Theological Department of Oberlin College to Chicago, with its Professors and funds. With the immigrant drift, ministers educated at Oberlin had come to Michigan and further west. In consequence, many of the churches in the Northwest felt a warm interest in Oberlin, yet were officially connected with the Seminary at Chicago, through the Triennial Convention. This division of interest was a chief reason for the proposed transfer. Concentration of strength, more work for the same Professors, and facilities for experimental work afforded by a large city, were also urged.

To these reasons it was replied:—That from the founding of Oberlin one of its aims was the education of ministers;—that there were doubts as to the legality of such a transfer; —and that, though the Chicago Seminary had a large work to do in its broad field of the Northwest, the Oberlin Seminary had a work to do in training ministers to labor in the opening fields of the South. Yet that, if the churches in Ohio did not put the Seminary at Oberlin in a more effectual way of reaching its ends, the proposed transfer would hereafter receive more favorable consideration.

XII.

TREASURERS, AGENTS AND GENERAL FUNDS.

At the organization of the Board of Directors, Philo Carpenter, Esq., was elected Treasurer. The pressure of his business forbade his serving. At the meeting of the Board in March, 1855, Lucius D. Olmsted, Esq., was elected to that office, and served, gratuitously yet faithfully, till his death seven years later. He organized the Treasury Department, and initiated its admirable system of keeping accounts.

In April, 1862, Rev. Henry L. Hammond was elected Treasurer and General Agent, Mr. Kedzie's resignation of the latter office taking effect in July of that year. Mr. Hammond served till July, 1872. Under his administration very marked progress was made in securing endowments and in erecting the permanent buildings of the Seminary. In substantial prosperity, the ten years of his service was the most encouraging decade in the history of the Seminary to this date.

In July, 1872, Rev. George S. F. Savage, D.D., elected Treasurer at the previous meeting of the Board, entered upon the duties of that office, with great advantage to the Seminary and satisfaction to the Board, and with like acceptance serving to this date. Securing funds imperilled by the late financial depression, safely investing them, providing for claims on the treasury, caring for the welfare of the students and the safety of the buildings, made his vocation, like that of his predecessor, perplexing and onerous. Yet its duties have been well met. Also, by his large acquaintance he has made the Seminary widely and favorably known, thereby securing to it an encouraging increase of both General and Permanent Funds.

After the short and successful agency of Rev. Stephen Peet, terminating with his death, Rev. Adam S. Kedzie was elected General Agent, or Financial Secretary. After more than seven years of service he resigned. He has since in like way served the Seminary as the exigency of its affairs demanded, and is now in the eleventh year of his service as Financial Secretary. In this work of raising funds for the Seminary, special service for brief times has been rendered by Revs. N. H. Eggleston, James Hawley, Hiram Elmer, Philo R. Hurd, D.D., C. A. Leach, W. H. Daniels, J. W. Cass, E. Hildreth, and F. Wheeler.

Nominal assets to the amount of about $250,000 were obtained for the Seminary during eight years from the first organization of the Board of Directors. Here was a show of prosperity, betokening the deep interest which Northwestern Congregationalists felt in the Seminary. Much of this was in notes payable in five annual installments. Before these fell due, many found that in giving such notes they had followed the impulse of their hearts, rather than the counsels of their judgments.

Then came the commercial disasters of 1857, and a few years later the War of the Rebellion. Many makers of these notes had gone to the defense of their country—some never to return. Consequently, though an admirable system of collections was persistently pushed by the Treasurer, L. D. Olmsted, Esq., still, when that disheartening Triennial Convention of Oct., 1861, came, he was compelled to report as past due—

January 1, 1859,	-	-	-	-	- $28,177 20
" 1, 1860,	-	-	-	-	34,233 74
" 1, 1861,	-	-	-	-	- 39,569 65

Union Park subscriptions to the building fund, made by parties who in so doing were interested only in material improvements, came to pretty general failure—in some cases because the parties themselves had failed;—others sought excuse because elegant and costly buildings were not speedily erected. The Treasurer and Financial Secretary sifted the chaff out of this General Fund, and the valuable part left was hypothecated to pay different claimants upon the treasury.

Amid these disheartenments, mention should be made of the faith and steadfastness of the Professors. They had left desirable positions and ventured their temporal prosperity upon the "promises to pay" held by the Treasurer; so many of which, excusably or not, were found a snare. Though invited to attractive work elsewhere, the Professors held fast the places, into which it seemed the providence of God had called them, being confident that God and the churches would not let so great a work come to failure.

Yet it will be well to know how near to failure the Seminary came in 1861 and '62. The Treasurer could not pay the Professors, whose chief pecuniary reliance thus failed them. The depressing influences of the Triennial Convention of October, 1861, were felt deeply. These were the discouraging times in the War of the Rebellion, when for weary months the daily report came; "All quiet on the Potomac." The difficulty about the location was in its ugliest shape, the Board being bound to make payments, which failure of the General Fund and Location Fund made impossible. It was a time of rebuke. The Board held before them the question of suspension. But how could this be done, when the practical work of the Seminary was going on so successfully?

The Board felt this to be the most critical period in their history: but rather than take up the question of suspension, they took in hand the matter of reducing expenses, and of suffering loss by failure in payments on the location.

Then each of the Professors voluntarily made reduction of his salary to the amount of $500 per annum for three years. At the same time, 1861, appeal was made by the Board to the churches—renewed in 1862—for collections to pay the Professors and keep the Seminary at work. In response, the General Association of Michigan called on its churches for $1,000 a year; Iowa for $750 from its churches; Wisconsin for $1,000; Illinois, outside of Chicago Association, $1,000; and the Chicago Association for $2,000. The results of these efforts were very disheartening. Meantime, a special form of note was pushed by the Agents, for a fund to be exclusively used in paying the Professors.

By all these means it was hoped $6,000 a year might be secured, but in consequence only $4,000 per year came. In the summer vacation of 1862, at the request of the Board of Directors, the Professors went East and appealed to friends in New England, and secured relief to the amount of about $4,000. And so, by one means and another, through the good providence of God, the Seminary, despite forebodings of evil and prophecies of failure, was kept alive, and the Professors at their posts, till the work of endowing three Professorships was successfully undertaken.

XIII.

ENDOWMENTS.

The Board of Directors held that, while endowments for Professorships and Scholarships were important, the first and most pressing object was a General Fund, all of which could be used for any of the purposes of the Seminary: consequently, to secure such a Fund was the chief aim in the early years of the Seminary. Yet, during the Agency of Mr. Kedzie, some scholarships were secured, which afterwards became available; and some Professorships, which did not become available for that purpose.

As before noted, Willard Keyes, Esq., of Quincy, Ill., gave land lying in that city, the prospective value of which, it was hoped, would endow the Chair of Ecclesiastical History. To meet a more immediate want of the Seminary, by his consent, this donation was used in erecting "Keyes Hall."

As early as in 1855, when the Seminary could be seen only by faith, Philo Carpenter, Esq., of Chicago, gave a donation of land in that city, the avails of which, when needed, were expected to be adequate to endow the Chair of Biblical Theology. This, with his consent, was used for other purposes of the Seminary.

And here it may be worth noting, as indicating the forces at work, that Mr. Carpenter stipulated, in accordance with the Constitution of the Seminary, that, when his offered endowment should become available, no incumbent of that Chair of Biblical Theology should teach that slavery is in accordance with the Word of God. Looking back from that time, this seemed a wise caution, however it may now appear. Perhaps there was no need of it in a Seminary controlled by the free churches of the North-west; but the stipulation, and its ready acceptance by the Directors, show the conflict of those times, and the spirit of the Founders of the Seminary.

For five years after the opening of the Seminary, its two, and then three Professors, were paid, and other expenses of the Institution met, from the General Fund. When this Fund ran low, and the discouragements of 1861 and '62 had been borne unto weariness, and even faintness, God stirred up the heart of Philo Carpenter, as before, to come to the relief of the Seminary. Compre-hending the situation and its peril, Mr. Carpenter, at his own instance, offered to give $5,000 to each of the three earliest occupied Professorships, on condition that the Board raise $20,000 additional for each of said Professor-ships; a pledge which he afterwards fully redeemed by paying the promised amount into the treasury in cash and United States bonds.

Encouraged by this offer, the friends of the Semi-nary, without seeing very clearly how the above con-dition could be met, nevertheless projected the plan of raising one of these Professorships in Illinois, a second in Michigan, Indiana and Wisconsin, and the third in New England. Manifold failures in finance had brought the friends of the Seminary to a spirit of moderation in their expectations.

Just then relief and encouragement came. In the spring of 1863, Prof. Fisk was called to labor in the Plymouth Church, Milwaukee, Wis., during a time of re-ligious interest. He won their hearts, and they took hold of the work of endowing his Professorship. In that and neighboring churches, Prof. Fisk raised $20,000, and $3,000 more among his friends in Boston, Mass., thereby

securing Mr. Carpenter's offer. This Wisconsin endowment, productive and unproductive, now amounts to
$35,000.

Encouraged by this marked success, Prof. Bartlett,
having secured $5,000 in Illinois, chiefly from the New
England Church, in Chicago, of which he had formerly
been Pastor, made three trips to the East, in 1863, and
canvassed in twenty-one towns and cities, aided in this by
the Treasurer, Rev. H. L. Hammond. Thereby, $20,000
and the pledge of Mr. Carpenter were secured. This
New England endowment, productive and unproductive,
now is $36,000.

Meantime, Prof. Haven, in 1863, by personal solicitation among his friends at the East, by canvass of St.
Louis, Mo., Terre Haute, Ind., and of the principal towns
in Illinois, aided in this by the Treasurer and others,
adding Mr. Carpenter's donation, secured the Illinois endowment, now amounting to $27,500 productive and un-
productive.

So inspiriting was the success in securing these
endowments, that the Triennial Convention, in April,
1864, was a jubilant one, quite in contrast with that of
October, 1861. When the Report of the Board of Directors was half read, the Convention felt constrained to
request that the reading might cease, till they could give
special thanks to God for these marked tokens of His
favor to the Seminary.

The churches in Michigan, meantime, began to feel
a sense of their responsibility in the matter of endowing
the Professorship of Ecclesiastical History. Nothing,
however, was done till 1866. Two years later, they addressed themselves more vigorously to the work, districting
ing the State, and assigning one district to each of the

resident Directors, to be canvassed by him. Blank forms of notes were prepared; also circulars, setting forth the main facts and arguments of the case. What the result of the effort would have been, cannot now be known; for just at this juncture the whole proceeding was stopped by the well-warranted announcement that Mrs. Mary J. Sweetzer, of Port Huron, Mich., had left a legacy of $30,000 for the endowment of the Professorship of Ecclesiastical History in the Chicago Theological Seminary, the same being one-third of the amount left by her for the religious department of life's business.

Mrs. Sweetzer was a worthy member of the Congregational Church at Port Huron, whose Pastor was Rev. J. S. Hoyt, D. D., a warm friend of the Seminary, a member of the Board of Visitors, and afterward of the Board of Directors. How far he quickened this interest in her mind, and how far the prevalent feeling among the churches of the State affected her, has been inquired for; but some one's modesty refuses to tell. The last $4,500 of this legacy will be paid in November, 1879, when the Sweetzer and Michigan endowments, productive and unproductive, will be $32,000.

Afterward, Iowa, not consenting to be without share in this good work, began the endowment of the Professorship of Pastoral Theology and Special Studies. This Iowa endowment now amounts to $25,000, of which only $19,000 are productive.

There are wanted: 1st. The completion of these well-begun endowments; 2d. An endowment for the Professorship of New Testament Literature; 3d. A fund for instruction in Elocution; and 4th. Foundations for certain much-desired Lectureships, thereby to enlarge the course of study. These are the pressing wants in the Department of Instruction.

Since the first, other Scholarships have been obtained. Of those already secured, twenty-one are productive:— viz., Austin Memorial, Horace Billings, Elizabeth Booth, Joseph Burrage, John L. Childs, Willard Cook, E. W. Davis, Deer Park, Depew, Emily Doane, John Dove, J. Worcester Field, Haywood, W. Hunt, L. J. Knowles, New London, Olivet, R. G. Peters, Joseph Tilson, Elbridge Torrey, W. Wolcott. Twelve other Scholarships are pledged for the future:—viz., Bascom, Blood, Cushing, Foster, Hubbell, Kendrick, Lewis, Mack, Reynolds, C. L. A. Tank, L. Warner and S. Warner.

The total amount of Scholarship Funds, paid and pledged, is $42,785. An urgent want of the Seminary is more of these funds. Yearly, students, who would prefer to study in our Seminary, are compelled to desist or go elsewhere, for lack of such aid. The founder of a Scholarship educates a perpetual line of young men for the ministry. Also, Scholarship Funds are needed, to afford the means and incentive to more extended study and riper scholarship. For coming conflicts, men cannot be educated too soon, nor too well.

Rev. W. W. Patton, D. D., President of Howard University, formerly an efficient member of the Board of Directors, gave $1,000, the interest of which is to be used in binding books, pamphlets, &c., for the Library. By vote of the Board, it is known as the " Patton Binding Fund."

In all such Institutions, a Permanent General Fund, the avails of which shall meet incidental, current and ever recurrent expenses, is a pressing necessity. The larger and wealthier an Institution becomes, the more urgent is this want. Dr. Savage, during his service as Treasurer, in addition to his other duties, has devoted his efforts, so far as he has had time, to raising such a fund, and has secured nearly $20,000 for that object. Toward this permanent General Fund, A. P. Kelley, C. F. Gates, and O. B. Green, Esqs., of Chicago, and John Bertram, Esq., of Salem, Mass., have made liberal donations. The completion of this fund would save much painful friction. No want of the Seminary is more constantly felt.

XIV.

OUT OF THE FIRE.

God is to be praised for His wonderful care of the Institution during the " Great Fire of Oct. 8th and 9th, 1871." He restrained the flames and kept them more than a mile away from the Seminary, in whose buildings some of its best friends found a safe refuge for their goods. The dwellings of the Professors were all passed by unharmed. The Treasurer's office was indeed burned, with important records, account books and documents, but the most valuable papers in it were saved.

A kind Providence had detained the Treasurer, Rev. H. L. Hammond, in the city, against his plans and wishes, over that eventful Sabbath. He was awakened at his home on Sangamon street, a mile and a half from the office, a little before 2 o'clock on Monday morning, and learned from a passer-by that the fire had crossed the river and was raging on the South side. He went out at once with his son to see it. Soon it became apparent that the office was in danger; and the valuables there, protected only by

an old safe, were in peril. They started for it. The devour-
ing wave had cut off their nearest route; but by making
a detour of several blocks, running through a storm of
live coals, they reached the office, 84 Washington street
near Dearborn, a few minutes before it was burned.

By the light of the flames, now close upon them,
they opened the safe, took out papers representing about
$150,000 of assets, hastily gathered a few other things,
and retreated amid the rush and roar of the hot wind and
flying fire-brands, the crash of falling walls and terrific
explosions, whose cause they could only conjecture.

But how to return to the West side? Five minutes
had rapidly spread the devastation east and north, and a
larger circuit was required for safety. They went east to
State street and north to South Water, before they could
turn westward and cross by Lake street bridge. They
regained Sangamon street safely, with their precious bur-
den, at three o'clock, having gone more than three miles
in one hour, an hour in which millions of dollars vanished,
and thousands of homes were destroyed.

This rescue not only required that the Treasurer and
his son should rush into danger, but the exertion necessary
to save those assets, induced severe suffering, and imperilled the life of the Treasurer. The importance of the
rescue was enhanced by the fact that the official records
of these securities was destroyed by the burning of the
County Records. It was found, after the fire, that,
although the investments of the Seminary's funds were
almost wholly in Chicago, only $2,000 were secured on
property in the burnt district; and that loan was soon
paid.

XV.

FACULTY AND STUDENTS.

Eight Professors have been elected, and seven in-augurated, in the Seminary. Rev. Joseph Haven, D. D. to the Chair of Systematic Theology, and Rev. Samuel C. Bartlett, D. D. to the Chair of Biblical Literature, were elected April 28th, 1858; and were inaugurated, the former October 20th, and the latter October 21st, of that year. These inaugurations were in the First Baptist Church, where now stands the Chamber of Commerce, and during the sessions of the Triennial Convention. To these Professors the Charge was given by Rev. Dr. Kitchel, as President of the Board. Prof. Haven gave instruction till the summer of 1870, when, while absent in Europe in search of health, he resigned his Chair. Prof. Bartlett resigned, to take effect July 1st, 1877, and accepted the Presidency of Dartmouth College.

Rev. Franklin W. Fisk, D. D. was elected April 2d, 1856, to the Chair of Sacred Rhetoric. Upon acceptance, after somewhat protracted consideration, he felt that he could not honorably release himself from Beloit College till 1859, and was inaugurated April 28th, of that year. The Charge was addressed to him by Rev. Dr. Bascom.

Rev. James T. Hyde, D. D., was elected Sept. 21st, 1869, to the Professorship of Pastoral Theology and Spe-cial Studies, and was inaugurated April 26th, 1870. The Charge by Rev. Dr. Robbins.

To the Chair resigned by Prof. Haven, Rev. George N. Boardman, D. D., was elected April 4th, 1871, and was inaugurated Sept. 14th, 1871. The Charge was deliv-ered by Rev. A. S. Kedzie.

Rev. Theodore W. Hopkins, A. M., was elected Professor of Ecclesiastical History April 29th, 1874, and was inaugurated April 29th, 1875. The Charge by Rev. Dr. Post.

Rev. Samuel Ives Curtiss, Ph. D.-D. D., was elected Professor of Biblical Literature, in the place of Dr. Bartlett, May 15th, 1878. He was inaugurated April 22d, 1879. The Charge by Rev. Dr. Chapin.

All the above inaugurations were, as required by the Constitution, in the presence of the Board of Directors, and with assent to the Constitutional Formula of Faith.

The Professorship of Biblical Literatue was divided June 10th, 1879. Whereupon Prof. S. Ives Curtiss, Ph. D.-D. D., was retained as the New England Professor of Old Testament Literature and Interpretation; and Prof. J. T. Hyde, D. D., was transferred to the Professorship of New Testament Literature and Interpretation, upon the Iowa Endowment.

At the same date, Rev. G. Buckingham Willcox, D. D., was elected to be Professor of Pastoral Theology and Special Studies. He has accepted and will enter upon his course of instruction in the autumn of 1879.

Prof. Edward M. Booth, A. M., has given instruction in elocution each year, since 1868, training all the students in the best methods of effective address.

Profs. Bartlett and Fisk, after many years of service, were granted leave of absence for a year, to travel and study in the Old World.

Special Courses of Lectures have been given by:—

1. Pres. J. M. Sturtevant, D. D., in 1859-62, on Modern Sects.

2. Rev. T. M. Post, D. D., in 1870–72, on Ecclesiastical History.

3. Rev. E. Beecher, D. D., in 1860–63, on Christian Organization of Society.

4. Rev. J. Blanchard, in 1858–59, on Connection of Old and New Testaments, and on Pastoral Theology.

5. Rev. J. B. Walker, D. D., in 1858–62, on Connection of Science and Religion.

6. Rev. A. L. Chapin, D. D., in 1862, on Christianity and Social Life.

7. Rev. W. W. Patton, D. D., in 1875–77, on Modern Skepticism.

This enlargement of the range of study by Lecturers especially qualified to open new fields of research, is an example, which other like Institutions have followed; and they have pushed it even more successfully than this Seminary, owing to lack of funds has been able to do.

Four hundred and four students have been instructed in Chicago Seminary. They have come from 24 States and Territories of our Union, also from Canada, England, Ireland, Scotland, Wales, France, Germany, Holland, Iceland, Africa, and India. Of these students some completed their course elsewhere, and some failed for various reasons to take the prescribed curriculum of study. The 209 others have graduated, 164 from the Regular and 45 from the Special Course.

The Alumni have formed an Association for further progress in study. For the past fifteen years this Association has met at the Seminary, and, aided by the Professors and others, its members have taken in hand for discussion such matters of doctrine and practice as study and experience suggested, renewing their attachment to

their *Alma Mater*, and more fully qualifying themselves
for their work.

. Of the Alumni twelve have died. The others are
serving the Master in twenty-eight states and territories
of our Union and in nine foreign countries. They were
all loyal to their country in the War of the Rebellion,
several of them having served in the army; but what is
more than that, so far as known, they are loyal to the
Truth and true to the Master.

XVI.

CONCLUSION.

The work of founding and fostering our Theological
Seminary has brought about noteworthy results. Only
brief mention of some of these can here be made.

1. The Seminary has trained hundreds of men for
the ministry, for many of whom it has opened a way that
would not else have been found—a way that now stands
open to thousands more.

2. These sons of our Northwestern churches are
laboring at home and abroad, thereby giving the churches
a new sense of their work, doing and to be done, on the
fields of Home and Foreign Missions.

3. These churches, in becoming productive of a ministry, are coming into a more quickened sense of coöperation with the Master, enlarging the range of thought and
ennobling the aim of life.

4. In training a ministry, the churches are coming,
also, to a rectified judgment of the qualification of minis-

ters for the work and conflict in this land and in the coming time.

5. In the organization of the Seminary a great force has been established in this Northwest. There has been gathered and set at work sanctified Scholarship of a high order, stimulating, defensive and aggressive.

6. Through the Seminary are provided ways by which men of forecast and wealth can inaugurate forces which shall reach many generations with quickening, moulding and sanctifying power.

REPORT

ON THE

Quarter Centennial Fund,

By the Board of Directors to the Triennial Convention,
and its Action thereon.

Twenty-five years ago began the movement to found our Theological Seminary. At the end of this Quarter Century, we inquire—"What next? What aspects has the work of the Lord, meantime, assumed? What, in consequence, is his word of command to us?

Our field of work lies within our Congregationalism, actual and possible. And to us our Congregationalism means not merely a polity, but a system of doctrines, an historic faith, the entire gospel, as held by our fathers and received by their sons—varied, but only made more vital and vigorous by the increasing light and heat of the Sun of Righteousness—a Congregationalism embodied in churches of spiritually quickened membership and ministry, with their growing institutions and working forces.

Our Theological Seminary, in its Boards of Control, Oversight and Instruction, and in the Triennial Convention of the Churches, which directly or indirectly elects these Boards, represents the Congregationalism of these Northwestern States and Territories, twelve of them, enough for a mighty empire.

What is our actual and relative standing in the concrete Congregationalism of our country? Here in this vast territory, covered by the constituency of our Seminary, is the *growing* part of our Congregationalism. The roots of our growth run far to the East and find nutriment —which we acknowledge with gratitude and pride— yet the actual growth, largely increased by such nutriment, is most visible in this Northwest.

Though of the Congregational church-members in the United States we have only 23 per cent., yet during the year covered by the statistics in the last Year Book, we have 31 per cent. in the net gain of church members, and 36 per cent. of the increase in Sabbath school attendance.

This crescent state of Congregationalism in the Northwest—the growing condition of the work assigned us by the Master—is still further and more emphatically shown by this fact:—the net increase in the number of our churches during the year reported in the last Year Book was 56. Of these new churches, 10 are on the Pacific Slope, 43 on the field covered by the constituency of our Theological Seminary, including Michigan on the east and Wyoming on the west, and only three in the remainder of the United States.

The growth of Congregationalism—of our work—in the Northwest, is shown by a broader fact. When 25 years ago the first steps were taken to organize our Theological Seminary, there was possible to it a constituency of only 380 Churches, northwest from Ohio. Now, after a lapse of 35 years, the Churches in the Northwest forming the constituency of our Seminary exceed that number by more than 1000.

Now why this concentration of forces in these Northwestern States by our own, and correspondingly by other Christian churches? Why this swift execution in these processes of organization? No man, who both thinks and prays, need search long for an answer.

1. Because here are gathering immense forces, vast powers of wealth to be developed—agricultural, commercial, mining and manufacturing—forces too vast for the comprehension of any finite mind. God's claim to these, to the hearts and hands that wield them, these Christian churches of all sorts must maintain and make good.

2. Because, slowly but surely, toward this junction of the Valley of the Lakes with the Valley of the Mississippi is moving the center of the population of the United States.

3. Because here is freedom of thought, trammeled by no traditions, in the churches or out; insisting upon rehandling everything, settled or unsettled; participated in by many nationalities and schools, reverent and irreverent.

The main work assigned us by the Master to do in this Northwest, and for which we need a ministry adequate in numbers and qualifications, is the evangelization which we are carrying on in common with other Christian churches. Yet we have, in addition to this, a less important, but positive and characteristic work. First. To afford a basis for church organization, on which evangelical Christians of various antecedents can readily unite—this by the adaptation, flexibility and adequate efficiency of our polity, and by holding the word of God as the only authoritative Rule of Faith. Also, secondly. By the freedom of utterance found in our pulpits and in the entire range of our Congregational literature, to foster and conserve all that is valuable in the freedom of thought, demanded and inevitable in this Northwest.

To the work of our churches there are hindrances.

1. The needful unfolding of the material wealth of the Northwest has given an intense aggravation to world-

liness, shown not only in the push of enterprises, but also in ruinous extravagance, and in the wreck of both characters and fortunes. Bonanza kings, railroad kings, merchant princes, lordly bankers and masters in manufacture, rule society, making men satisfied with a prosperity which neither betters humanity, nor helps on the great ends for which the ages continue.

2. The hindrances become more formidable because to the dullness of carnality and the engrossment of worldliness there is added a various infidelity—among the educated a scientific skepticism—among the unlettered the gross infidelity of Thomas Paine—wrestling again with difficulties which well read men know were fully met 100 years ago.

3. Then there is Communism in its American shapes, young, but growing, and greedy of life, together with other evils of a society that is becoming stratified in a very undemocratic way and degree. This Communism and its allied craft-organizations, are likely to do something more than, as once, to stop the railroad traffic of the country.

4. Sectarianism, everywhere a hindrance, in instances, not a few, unpeaceably and unsafely dominant.

Only the Gospel, as it ennobles life with its hopes, as it tones society by its individual regenerations, shapes law and vitalizes human brotherhood, can cure sectarianism, and solve the problems, with which Communism and craft-organizations vainly struggle. Only the Gospel can make safe the prosperity of the Northwest.

So, for the work to be done in these Northwestern States, there is needed that right hand of the Churches, an educated, spiritual and orthodox ministry—men, who can find a place to work, or make a place—men, who by residence and education in this section of our country shall be in acquaintance and sympathy with the work here to be done—men, abreast with the best literature of their age; testing every moral question by the infallible Word of God; and, like Congregational ministers from the Plymouth Rock days till now, leaders in the thinking of their times. Every year the forces at work for good or evil grow stronger, so must the pulpit, or yield to such rivals as the platform and the press.

For the training of such a ministry—for the work urgent upon our Theological Seminary—it needs:

1. Completion in the endowment of the present Professorships.

2. An endowment of the Professorship of New Testament Literature.

3. The completion of the Permanent General Fund.

4. A Library Fund, large additions to the Library, and a fire-proof Library Hall.

5. Additional Scholarships:—all requiring at least $100,000.

Your Committee, therefore, could not be true to their own convictions, without urging these Resolutions:

1. That resting on the merits of the case, trusting in the Lord, and encouraged by the counsels and offers already made, as well as by the hopes we entertain, we, as a Board of Directors put in charge of this important Institution, ask the Churches, in grateful recognition of the work God has already given the Seminary to do, and of its greater work hereafter, to increase its endowments by raising a Quarter Centennial Fund of at least $100,-000, to be devoted to such wants of the Seminary as the donors of said Fund and the Board of Directors shall determine.

2. That this whole subject be laid before the Triennial Convention about to meet, asking its judgment thereon.

3. That if the Churches in Triennial Convention respond favorably to this request, the Board of Directors devote their efforts assiduously to the work of raising this Quarter Centennial Fund, till it be accomplished.

4. That for the purpose of more fully acquainting the Churches with the Seminary, and interesting them in its work, an abstract of a History of the Seminary to date, be published and distributed, supplemented by this Report, and such action as the Triennial Convention may take.

A. S. KEDZIE,
E. W. BLATCHFORD,   *Committee.*
J. W. SCOVILLE,
O. DAVIDSON,

In behalf of the Board of Directors, E. W. Blatchford, Esq., presented the above Report accompanying it with suitable remarks. It was then moved that the Report be amended so as to ask for $150,000 instead of $100.000. After full discussion, both the amendment and the Report were unanimously adopted by a rising vote.

May the Lord multiply those who shall have power to make this Seminary strong for the work it has to do in the future. May He give them wisdom to see how an enlargement of the Seminary's work will advance the Kingdom of Christ, at home and abroad. And by their liberal contribution to the Seminary's strength may He bring them into fuller fellowship with Him in work for the world's salvation.

CHARTER.

AN ACT

TO INCORPORATE THE CHICAGO THEOLOGICAL SEMINARY.

SECTION 1. *Be it enacted by the People of the State of Illinois, represented in the General Assembly,* That STEPHEN PEET, WILLIAM CARTER, FLAVEL BASCOM, M. A. JEWETT, GEORGE W. PERKINS, PHILO CARPENTER, TRUMAN POST, JOHN C. HOLBROOK, HORACE HOBART, JOHN J. MITER, HIRAM FOOTE, JOSEPH JOHNSTON, HARVEY D. KITCHEL, ALDEN B. ROBBINS, ADAM S. KEDZIE, L. SMITH HOBART, NATHANIEL H. EGGLESTON, SOLOMON L. WITHEY, JESSE GUERNSEY, JOSEPH E. BEEBE, CHAS. W. CAMP, JOHN G. FOOTE, RICHARD HALL, GEO. S. F. SAVAGE, and their successors, be and they hereby are created a body politic and corporate, to be styled, "The Board of Directors of the Chicago Theological Seminary," and by that name and style to remain and have perpetual succession, with full power to sue and be sued, plead and be impleaded, to acquire, hold and convey property, real and personal, to have and use a common seal, to alter and renew the same at pleasure, to make and alter a Constitution and By-Laws for the conducting and government of said Institution, and fully to do whatever may be necessary to carry out the object of this act of incorporation.

SECTION 2. That the Seminary shall be located in or near the City of Chicago. The object shall be to furnish instruction and the means of education to young men preparing for the Gospel Ministry, and the Institution shall be equally open to all denominations of Christians for this purpose.

SECTION 3. That the Board of Directors shall consist of twenty-four members, nine of whom shall constitute a quorum for the transaction of business. The Directors shall hereafter be elected in accordance with the provisions of the Constitution under which they act, and shall hold their office until their successors are appointed.

Section 4. That the Board of Directors shall have power to appoint an Executive Committee, and such agents as they may deem necessary, and such Officers, Professors and Teachers as the government and instruction of the Seminary may require, and prescribe their duties; to remove any of them for sufficient reasons, and to prescribe and direct the course of studies to be pursued in the Institution; also to confer such degrees as are consistent with the object of the Institution.

Section 5. That the property, of whatever kind or description, belonging or appertaining to said Seminary, shall be forever free and exempt from all taxation, for all purposes whatsoever.

Section 6. This act to take effect and be in force from and after its passage, and it shall be deemed a public act, and shall be construed liberally in all courts for the purposes therein expressed.

THOS. J. TURNER,
Speaker of the House of Representatives.

G. KOERNER,
Speaker of the Senate.

Approved February 15, 1855.
J. A. MATTESON.

UNITED STATES OF AMERICA, ⎱ ss.
STATE OF ILLINOIS. ⎰

I, Alexander Starne, Secretary of State of the State of Illinois, do hereby certify that the foregoing is a true and correct copy of an enrolled law now on file in my office.

In testimony whereof, I have hereunto set my hand
L. S.   and affixed the seal of said State, this 6th day of
March, A.D. 1855.

ALEXANDER STARNE,
Secretary of State.

ALUMNI.

NAMES.	GRADUATED.	ORDAINED.	RESIDENCE.
Abbott, C. H.	1875	Dec. 1875	Huntley, Ill.
Adams, William A.	1862	May 18, 1862	Deceased.
Anderson, David R.	1876	June 15, 1876	Oconomowoc, Wis.
Anderson, Kerr C.	1875	Nov. 11, 1873	Oshkosh, Wis.
Armstrong, Julius C.	1874	June 17, 1874	Lyonsville, Ill.
Arnold, Arthur E.	1867	Dec. 1867	Lemars, Ia.
Arnold, Seth A.	1873	Sept. 8, 1873	Wittenberg, Ia.
Allender, John	1868	Feb. 23, 1869	Red Oak, Ia.
Atkinson, John L.	1869	Sept. 24, 1869	Missionary to Japan.
Atkinson, William H.	1867	April 18, 1867	Orchard, Ia.
Bailey, Amos Judson	1871	Oct. 24, 1871	Hennepin, Ill.
Baird, John W.	1872	May 22, 1872	Missionary to Bulgaria.
Baker, Mons. Samuel	1879		Northfield, Minn.
Baldwin, David J.	1865	Nov. 10, 1865	Sibley, Ia.
Barnard, Elihu C.	1866	Dec. 18, 1866	Moline, Ill.
Barnes, Charles M.	1859	Sept. 16, 1859	Chicago, Ill.
Barnes, Henry E.	1864	May 28, 1864	Haverill, Mass.
Barrett, Edward N.	1870	Nov. 21, 1871	Chicago, Ill.
Barrett, John F.	1877	Dec. 21, 1877	Manchester, Ia.
Bascom, George S.	1870	June 29, 1870	Peru, Ill.
Beach, Edwin R.	1869	Sept. 21, 1869	Longmont, Colorado.
Beecher, Frederick W.	1861	Nov. 12, 1861	Jamestown, N. Y.
Beecher, George H.	1863	Oct. 26, 1864	Brooklyn, N. Y.
Benton, Ledyard E.	1874	Nov. 19, 1874	Crete, Neb.
Betts, Eben M.	1869	Sept. 19, 1869	Fond du Lac, Wis.
Bidwell, John B.	1874	June 17, 1874	Tomah, Wis.
Bill, A. Wesley	1873	Sept. 9, 1873	Menominee, Mich.
Bingham, Charles M.	1870	June 16, 1870	Milburn, Ill.
Bisbee, Marvin B.	1874	Sept. 10, 1874	Cambridgeport, Mass.
Blake, Daniel H.	1859	June 9, 1859	Deceased.
Blodgett, George D.	1861	May 8, 1861	Deceased.
Bradshaw, John W.	1874	Oct. 29, 1874	Batavia, Ill.
Bray, William L.	1861	Aug. 8, 1861	Clinton, Ia.
Breckenridge, Daniel M.	1869	Sept. 21, 1869	Fort Dodge, Ia.

NAMES.	GRADUATED.	ORDAINED.	RESIDENCE.
Bross, Harmon	1867	Sept. 1863	Crete, Neb.
Brobst, Flavius J	1879	1879	Roberts, Ill.
Brown, T. Lincoln	1873	Sept. 2, 1873	Elkhart, Ind.
Burton, Nathan L	1877	June 19, 1877	Lamoille, Ill.
Burt, Jirah S	1860		North Weston, Ind.
Bush, Frederick W	1871	May 16, 1871	Alamo, Mich.
Butcher, William R	1869	June 15, 1869	Kokomo, Ind.
Campbell, Gabriel	1868	Oct. 27, 1868	East Minneapolis, Minn.
Cass, John W	1863	May 11, 1863	Deceased.
Chamberlin, James A	1879	1879	Union Grove, Wis.
Champlin, Oliver P	1870	July 10, 1870	Sleepy Eye, Minn.
Chase, Edward R	1871		Deceased.
Cheeny, Russell L	1876	Oct. 24, 1876	Bloomington, Wis.
Chittenden, Albert J	1874		Boulder, Colorado.
Clapp, Cephas F	1871	June 21, 1871	Prairie du Chien, Wis.
Clark, William J	1869	Nov. 19, 1869	Okalla, Ill.
Clark, Moulton L	1877	1877	Constableville, N. Y.
Codington, George S	1870	July 1, 1870	Deceased.
Comstock, D. W	1864	June 5, 1861	Otsego, Mich.
Corsbie, Hadley M	1879	Aug. 31, 1876	Burlington, Wis.
Cragin, Charles C	1869	Feb. 16, 1870	McGregor, Ia.
Crawford, Matthew A	1878		David City, Neb.
Crawford, O. D	1872	Nov. 1, 1872	West Bloomfield, N. Y.
Cross, W. H	1870	June 29, 1870	Hollister, Cal.
Croswell, Micah S	1868	April 21, 1869	Amboy, Ill.
Cruzan, John Alexander	1871	Sept. 28, 1871	Portland, Oregon.
Curtis, Asher W	1868	July 2, 1868	Hastings, Neb.
Curtis, William Willis	1873	Aug. 10, 1873	Missionary to Japan.
Dada, Edgar P	1864	July 1, 1864	Mazeppa, Minn.
Daniels, Henry M	1861	June 25, 1861	Dallas, Texas.
Davis, Jerome D	1869	June 1, 1869	Missionary to Japan.
Day, Warren F	1866	May 2, 1866	East Saginaw, Mich.
Danforth, James R	1867	Jan. 2, 1868	Philadelphia, Pa.
Demarest, Sidney B.	1869	Sept. 7, 1869	Dartford, Wis.
Dewey, Willis C	1877	May 29, 1877	Missionary to Turkey.
Dickinson, C. E	1863	June 2, 1863	Elgin, Ill.
Dickinson, Samuel F	1869	June 9, 1870	Cambridge, Ill.
Dickenson, William G	1873	June 24, 1873	Shabbona, Ill.
Dixon, Julian Howell	1871	Sept. 6, 1871	Ridgefield, Ill.
Douglass, Francis J	1869	June 22, 1869	Richmond, Ill.
Douglas, Truman O	1868	Oct. 28, 1868	Osage, Ia.
Durham, Benjamin (M. D.)	1861		Chicago, Ill.
Durham, Henry (M. D.)	1863	Nov. 3, 1864	Crete, Neb.
Duncan, John C	1877		Tugaloo, Miss.
DeRiemer, William E	1867	April 18, 1867	Missionary to Ceylon.

NAMES.	GRADUATED.	ORDAINED.	RESIDENCE.
Edgerton, Foster E..........			Died just before graduating.
Evans, Samuel E............	1867	April 18, 1867	Seakonk, Rhode Island.
Fay, Osmer W.............. ..	1863	July 2, 1867	Montgomery, Ala.
Feemster, Paul S............	1867	Nov. 25,.1869	Columbus, Miss.
Ferner, John W..............	1876	June 17, 1876	Mitchelville, Ia.
Ferris, Hiram J.............	1876	Sept. 7, 1876	New Milford, Ill.
Fonda, Jesse Lawrence.......	1873	Sept. 16, 1873	Morris, Minn.
Fowle, Hanford	1866	June 13, 1866	East Troy, Wis.
Gallagher, Wm. Jr...........	1874	Dec. 1, 1874	Boston, Mass.
Gillespie, Thomas	1867	Nov. 20, 1867	Bristol, Wisconsin.
Gilmore, Daniel W..........	1875		Potosi, Wisconsin.
Goodell, Henry M...........	1874	1876	Newago, Mich.
Goodrich, Edward P.........	1870	Oct. 1, 1870	Decatur, Mich.
Goodsell, Dennis.............	1879		Fergus Falls, Minn.
Granger, John S.............	1866	July 12, 1866	Granville, Ill.
Guild, Rufus B..............	1864	Nov. 3, 1864	Seneca, Kan.
Guyton, Jacob F.............	1869	Aug. 24, 1869	Evanston, Ill.
Hall, Martin S..............	1871	June 15, 1871	Lawn Ridge, Ill.
Hand, Laroy S..............	1868	June 18, 1868	Ogden, Ia.
Harbaugh, Hiram Wallace ...	1879		Pecatonica, Ill.
Hardy, Vitellas M...........	1869	Jan. 31, 1872	West Randolph, Vt.
Harrah, Charles C..........	1870	Aug. 3, 1870	Galva, Ill.
Harrison, James.............	1868	Dec. 17, 1868	Wisconsin.
Harvey, Charles A..........	1861	June 20, 1861	Middletown, N. Y.
Hancock, Charles (M. D.)....	1861	June 5, 1861	Alden, Iowa.
Hibbard, Charles	1869	Sept. 21, 1869	Fairmount, Neb.
Higley, George T............	1861	May 31, 1861	Ashland, Mass.
Hildreth, Edward	1861	Dec. 30, 1862	Chicago, Ill.
Hill, Dexter D..............	1869	June 1, 1869	Aurora, Ill.
Hinckley, William H.........	1877	Dec. 20, 1876	Racine, Wis.
Holcombe, Gilbert T.........	1875	June 22, 1875	California.
Holbrook, David L..........	1877	July 19, 1877	Geneva, Wis.
Hooker, Edward T..........	1867	June 17, 1868	Castleton, Vt.
Humphrey, C. C.............	1861	June 6, 1861	Osceola, Neb.
Hughes, Isaac Collstr........	1873	Sept. 21, 1873	Columbus City, Ia.
Hurd, Alva Ansel	1871	Mar. 21, 1871	Scotland, Conn.
Jacobs, Henry..............	1870	Sept. 22, 1870	Wayne Center, Ill.
Jagger, Edward L...........	1861	Mar. 6, 1862	Bristol, N. H.
Jones, David D..............	1875		Minnesota.
Jones, Lemuel......	1864	April 20, 1865	Englewood, N. J.
Keen, Lyman S..............	1879	-	Wauponsie Grove, Ill.
Kirk, Robert	1874	Sept. 1874	Springfield, Dakota.
Knobel, Godfrey C..........	1875	April 11, 1875	Philadelphia, Pa.

NAMES.	GRADUATED.	ORDAINED.	RESIDENCE.
Landon, George M...........	1868	1868	Monroe, Mich.
Lathrop, Stanley E..........	1870	Dec. 21, 1870	Macon, Ga.
Lewis, Edwin N.............	1862	Oct. 14, 1862	Ottawa, Ill.
Marsh, Charles E............	1867	Oct. 13, 1868	Summer Hill, Ill.
Marsh, George Daniel........	1871	July 1872	Missionary to Bulgaria.
Matson, Albert..............	1871		Salina, Kan.
May, Oscar G...............	1870	June 21, 1870	Fulton, Wis.
McArthur, H. G.............	1859.	Aug. 25, 1859	Beloit, Wis.
McCulloch, Oscar C..........	1870	Oct. 19, 1870	Indianapolis, Ind.
Merrill, Chas. Wilber........	1873	Oct. 29, 1873	Spring Valley, Minn.
Millard, Watson B...........	1874	June 18, 1874	Dundee, Ill.
Miller, Richard.............	1873	Dec. 23, 1873	Calumet, Mich.
Millerd, Norman A..........	1862	June 27, 1862	Chicago, Ill.
Mills, Harlow S.............	1877	June 5, 1877	Dunlap, Iowa.
Mirick, Edward A...........	1869	Sept. 19, 1869	Neodesha, Kan.
Montgomery, John A........	1866	June 15, 1866	Morris, Ill.
Morrill, Stephen S...........	1859	May 12, 1859	Deceased.
Nelson, Geo. William........	1873	Sept. 9, 1873	Wauwatosa, Wis.
Norcross, Lanson P..........	1869	Jan. 26, 1870	Deadwood, Wyo. Terr.
Northcott, Theodore C.......	1875	May 13, 1875	Faribault, Minn.
Norton, Frank B.............	1864	July 12, 1864	Oshkosh, Wis.
Noyes, Mortimer L. S........	1871		Deceased Nov. 14, 1872.
Oakley, James..............	1875	Oct. 31, 1875	Ridgefield, Ill.
Paddock, George A..........	1868	Aug. 20, 1868	Deceased.
Parker, Homer Joseph.......	1873	Sept. 16, 1873	Bay City, Mich.
Parker, John D.............	1865	Aug. 16, 1865	Kansas City, Mo.
Philips, Wm. Irving..........	1876	Sept. 1, 1876	College Springs, Ia.
Pinkerton, Myron W.........	1871	Aug. 1871	Missionary to South Africa.
Putnam, Samuel P...........	1868		Ohio.
Reed, Charles Francis........	1873	June 1, 1874	
Reed, Myron W.............	1866	July 10, 1866	Indianapolis, Ind.
Rice, Augustus M............	1873		Little Compton, R. I.
Richards, J. P..............	1861	Oct. 31, 1861	Bowensburg, Ill.
Riggs, Alfred L.............	1862	Nov. 4, 1863	Miss'y Santee Agency, Neb.
Riggs, T. L................	1872	Jan. 17, 1873	Miss'y Ft. Sully, Dakota.
Rindell, Gilbert, Jr..........	1874	Nov. 1874	Plymouth, Wis.
Robbins, H. H.............	1874	July 29, 1874	Postville, Ia.
Rogers, Charles H..........	1877	July, 11, 1877	Lansing, Ia.
Root, Barnabas Walker......	1873	Nov. 1874	Deceased.
Safford, Albert Walker.......	1871	Aug. 2, 1872	Vermont.
Samuel, Robert.............	1859	Nov. 3, 1859	Cawker City, Kan.
Sanders, Clarendon M........	1867	April 19, 1867	Cheyenne, Wyo. Terr.
Sargent, Moses F............	1879		Winnebago, Ill.
Shinn, Robert F.............	1865	Sept. 14, 1868	Chicago, Ill.

NAMES.	GRADUATED.	ORDAINED.	RESIDENCE.
Shirrill, Dana	1873	June 24, 1873	Forest, Ill.
Simmons, H. C.	1872	May 8, 1872	Marshall, Minn.
Skeels, Henry M.	1876	June 29, 1876	Turner, Ill.
Skentlebury, Wm. H.	1873	July 7, 1875	Wacousta, Mich.
Smith, Andrew J.	1874	July 1, 1874	Neosho, Mo.
Smith, Augustine T.	1866		Deceased.
Smith, Emerson F.	1875		Wellsville, Kan.
Smith, Frederick H.	1877		Crookston, Minn.
Smith, James F.	1873	May 6, 1873	Crete, Ill.
Smith, George	1867	Jan. 20, 1868	Whitewater, Wis.
Smith, Orville S.	1874	Nov. 4, 1874	Hartland, Wis.
Smith, Simon P.	1879		Marietta, Ga.
Storm, Julius E.	1875	June 9, 1875	Princeton, Minn.
Stratton, Samuel F.	1868	Sept. 24, 1868	Downer's Grove, Ill.
Sveinbjorson, Arnabjarni	1878		Reykjarvik, Iceland.
Tade, Ewing O.	1861	Sept. 4, 1861	Fidalgo, Wash. Ter.
Taylor, John G.	1872	Jan. 9, 1873	Melrose, Mass.
Thain, Alexander R.	1870	Oct. 17, 1870	Galesburg, Ill.
Thayer, Carmi C.	1867	April 18, 1867	Maywood, Ill.
Tibbitts, Dallas David	1873		Blackberry, Ill.
Todd, Quintus C.	1879		Corning, Ia.
Tompkins, James	1867	April 24, 1867	Chicago, Ill.
Towle, Charles A.	1869	May 29, 1869	Chicago, Ill.
Tuttle, Hanson Bascom	1873	Jan. 20, 1874	Worthington, Minn.
Van Noorden, Emmanuel	1871	Oct. 1873	Miss'y to Buenos Ayres, S. A.
Van Wagner, Allen J.	1873	Oct. 23, 1873	Elmwood, Ill.
Volentine, Thomas J.	1870	Oct. 13, 1870	Webster's Grove, Mo.
Wainwright, G. W.	1862	May 27, 1862	Raymond, Wis.
Waterman, William A.	1867	Feb. 13, 1868	Marion, Ia.
Waterman, H. B.	1869	June 1869	Moline, Ill.
Webb, Stephen W.	1869	April 19, 1870	Great Falls, N. H.
Wells, George H.	1867	Oct. 1, 1867	Montreal, Canada.
Wells, Spencer R.	1867	April 18, 1867	Miss'y Armednugger, India.
West, Lester L.	1878	Nov. 13, 1878	Fort Dodge, Ia.
Wheeler, Charles H.	1867	1867	Ohio.
Wheeler, Frederick	1861	Feb. 18, 1862	Hoylton. Ill.
Wiard, H. De Forrest	1878	Nov. 11, 1873	Eadville, Ill.
Wilcox, Seth M.	1875	Dec. 1875	Griggsville, Ill.
Williams, Edward M.	1868	Feb. 25, 1869	Minneapolis, Minn.
Willett, Mahlon	1873	June 4, 1873	San Jose, Cal.
Wilson, Henry	1876	Jan. 4, 1877	Wyanet, Ill.
Wright, Eugene F.	1876	Nov. 1875	Seward, Ill.
Yates, Thomas	1872	Sept. 1, 1874	Shultzburg, Mass.

THE CHICAGO THEOLOGICAL SEMINARY

LOCATED AT THE

Corner of Ashland and Warren Avenues, *opposite Union Park.*

It was incorporated by the Illinois Legislature, in 1855, as "THE BOARD OF DIRECTORS OF THE CHICAGO THEOLOGICAL SEMINARY."

☞ The full corporate name should be used in all Notes, Deeds and Bequests.

BOARD OF DIRECTORS:

E. W. BLATCHFORD, Esq., *President* ....Chicago.
REV. T. M. POST, D. D., *Vice-President*.........................St. Louis, Mo.
REV. G. S. F. SAVAGE, D. D., *Secretary*...Chicago.

CLASS I.—Term of Office Expires in 1882.

REV. A. S. KEDZIE...St. Joseph, Mich.
REV. N. A. HYDE, D. D.,.......................................Indianapolis, Ind.
REV. F. BASCOM, D. D.,..Hinsdale, Ill.
REV. E. P. GOODWIN, D. D......................................Chicago.
REV. G. S. F. SAVAGE, D. D......................................"
E. W. BLATCHFORD, Esq..."
J. W. SCOVILLE, Esq...Oak Park, Ill.
REV. A. L. CHAPIN, D. D...Beloit, Wis.
REV. H. T. ROSE...Milwaukee, Wis.
J. H. MERRILL, Esq..Des Moines, Iowa.
REV. H. N. GATES...Omaha, Neb.
REV. PETER M. VICKER, D. D......................................Topeka, Kan.

CLASS II.—Term of Office Expires 1885.

REV. O. C. THOMPSON ....Detroit, Mich.
REV. W. F. DAY..East Saginaw, Mich.
R. G. PETERS, Esq...Manistee, Mich.
C. G. HAMMOND, Esq..Chicago, Ill.
L. G. FISHER, Esq.."
O. DAVIDSON, Esq...Elgin, Ill.
REV. C. W. CAMP...Waukesha, Wis.
REV. A. B. ROBBINS, D. D.......................................Muscatine, Iowa.
REV. G. F. MAGOUN, D. D...Grinnell, Iowa.
J. G. FOOTE, Esq...Burlington, Iowa.
REV. J. W. STRONG, D. D...Northfield, Minn.
REV. T. M. POST, D. D...St. Louis, Mo.

EXECUTIVE COMMITTEE:

J. W. SCOVILLE, Esq., *Chairman.*   REV. G. S. F. SAVAGE, D. D., *Secretary.*
E. W. BLATCHFORD, Esq.   REV. E. P. GOODWIN, D. D.
REV. F. BASCOM, D. D.   L. G. FISHER, Esq.
                        O. DAVIDSON, Esq.

BOARD OF VISITORS:

CLASS I.—Term of Office Expires 1882.

REV. J. W. BRADSHAW..Batavia, Ill.
REV. E. M. WILLIAMS..Minneapolis, Minn.
REV. J. G. MERRILL..Davenport, Iowa.
REV. D. L. HOLBROOK..Geneva, Wis.

CLASS II.—Term of Office Expires 1885.

PRES. JAMES B. ANGELL, LL. D....................................Ann Arbor, Mich.
REV. G. T. LADD...Milwaukee, Wis.
REV. E. F. WILLIAMS...Chicago, Ill.
REV. E. KENT...Michigan City, Ind.

AUDITING COMMITTEE:

LYMAN BAIRD, Esq..Chicago, Ill.
C. F. GATES, Esq..."
GEO. CULVER, Esq..."

FACULTY:

REV. F. W. FISK, D. D., *Wisconsin Professor of Sacred Rhetoric.*
REV. J. T. HYDE, D. D., *Professor of New Testament Literature.*
REV. G. N. BOARDMAN, D. D., *Illinois Professor of Systematic Theology.*
REV. T. W. HOPKINS, A. M., *Sweetser & Michigan Professor of Ecclesiastical History*
REV. S. IVES CURTISS, PH.D., D.D., *New England Prof. of Old Testament Literature*
REV. G. B. WILLCOX, D. D., *Professor of Pastoral Theology & Special Studies.*
E. M. BOOTH, *Instructor in Elocution.*
PROF. G. N. BOARDMAN, D. D., *Librarian.*

REV. A. S. KEDZIE, FINANCIAL SECRETARY.
REV. G. S. F. SAVAGE, D. D., TREASURER.

OFFICE: 112 WEST WASHINGTON STREET,
CHICAGO, ILL.

www.ingramcontent.com/pod-product-compliance
Lightning Source LLC
Chambersburg PA
CBHW021533270326
41930CB00008B/1230